DIGITAL DATA SECURITY

Heather C. Hudak

CRABTREE
PUBLISHING COMPANY
WWW.CRABTREEBOOKS.COM

Author: Heather C. Hudak
Series research and development:
    Reagan Miller
Editor-in-chief: Lionel Bender
Editor: Ellen Rodger
Proofreaders: Laura Booth,
    Melissa Boyce
Project coordinator: Petrice Custance
Design and photo research: Ben White
Production: Kim Richardson
**Production coordinator and
    prepress technician:** Tammy McGarr
Print coordinator: Katherine Berti
Consultant: Emily Drew,
    The New York Public Library

Produced for Crabtree
Publishing Company by
Bender Richardson White

Photographs and reproductions:
Alamy: 8–9 (Xinhua), 11 (Kathy deWitt), 20 (Radim
Beznoska), 28 (imageBROKER), 29 (Hero Images
Inc), 40–41 (RosaIreneBetancourt); Getty Images: 4–5
(Andrew Harrer/Bloomberg), 7 (Chip Somodevilla),
21 (Philippe Huguen), 24–25 (Roberto Machado Noa/
LightRocket), 33 (Vadim Savitsky/TASS), 36–37 (Robert
Nickelsberg); Shutterstock: 1 (Andrey_Popov), 6 (Milles
Studio), 10–11 (pandpstock001), 12–13 top (fizkes), 12–13
bottom (Georgejmclittle), 14–15 (Gorodenkoff), 18–19 top
(solarseven), 18–19 bottom (PR Image Factory), 22–23
(Jarretera), 23 (StreetVJ), 26–27 top (rawpixel.com), 26–27
bottom (Toria), 30–31 top (think4photop), 30–31 bottom
(Prostock–studio), 34 top (Diabluses), 34 bottom (Twin
Design), 35 (Wachiwit), 37 (Rob Crandall), 38 (sdecoret),
38–39 (Suwin), 42–43 (LeonidKos); Topfoto: 16–17 (PA
Photos), 17 (M.Berman/ClassicStock); Icons & heading
band: shutterstock.com
Diagrams: Stefan Chabluk, using the following as
sources of data: p 7. Statista.com, p 12. Statista.com,
p. 23 Pandasecurity.com/Verizon 2017 Data Breach
Investigations Report, p. 30 Gallup.com, p. 32 Statista.
com/U.S. Federal government figures, p. 39 Barkly.com/
Ponemon Institute, p. 40 Barkly.com/Ponemon Institute,
p. 43 Pew Research Center

Library and Archives Canada Cataloguing in Publication

Hudak, Heather C., 1975-, author
        Digital data security / Heather C. Hudak.

(Get informed -- stay informed)
Includes bibliographical references and index.
Issued in print and electronic formats.
ISBN 978-0-7787-5331-5 (hardcover).--
ISBN 978-0-7787-5345-2 (softcover).--
ISBN 978-1-4271-2192-9 (HTML)

        1. Internet--Security measures--Juvenile literature.
2. World Wide Web--Security measures--Juvenile literature.
3. Web sites--Security measures--Juvenile literature.
4. Online social networks--Security measures--Juvenile literature.
5. Internet and children--Juvenile literature. 6. Computer crimes--
Juvenile literature. I. Title.

TK5105.59.H84 2019   j005.8   C2018-905644-4
                                                                     C2018-905645-2

Library of Congress Cataloging-in-Publication Data

Names: Hudak, Heather C., 1975- author.
Title: Digital data security / Heather C. Hudak.
Description: New York : Crabtree Publishing, [2019] | Series: Get
    informed--stay informed |
    Includes bibliographical references and index.
Identifiers: LCCN 2018057988 (print) |
    LCCN 2019001270 (ebook) |
    ISBN 9781427121929 (Electronic) |
    ISBN 9780778753315 (hardcover : alk. paper) |
    ISBN 9780778753452 (pbk. : alk. paper)
Subjects: LCSH: Computer crimes--Prevention--Juvenile literature.
    | Computer security--Juvenile literature.
Classification: LCC HV6773 (ebook) |
    LCC HV6773 .H83 2019 (print) | DDC 005.8--dc23
LC record available at https://lccn.loc.gov/2018057988

Crabtree Publishing Company

www.crabtreebooks.com   1-800-387-7650

Printed in the U.S.A./032019/CG20190118

Published in Canada
Crabtree Publishing
616 Welland Ave.
St. Catharines, ON
L2M 5V6

Published in the United States
Crabtree Publishing
PMB 59051
350 Fifth Avenue, 59th Floor
New York, NY 10118

Published in the United Kingdom
Crabtree Publishing
Maritime House
Basin Road North, Hove
BN41 1WR

Published in Australia
Crabtree Publishing
Unit 3 – 5 Currumbin Court
Capalaba
QLD 4157

CONTENTS

Unknown to you, someone, somewhere, may be reading the emails you send, noting the websites and YouTube videos you view, copying your homework, and gathering your friends' phone numbers, email addresses, and photos from your smartphone. All day, every day, **cybercriminals** known as hackers are trying to extract information from computers and computing devices. This information is known as digital data. Unless you take steps to secure your data, it can be available to everyone.

*The diverse threats we face are increasingly cyber-based. Much of America's most sensitive data is stored on computers. We are losing data, money, and ideas through cyber **intrusions**. This threatens innovation and, as citizens, we are also increasingly **vulnerable** to losing our personal information.*

James Comey Jr., former director of the U.S. Federal Bureau of Investigation (FBI)

▲ At a news conference on March 15, 2017, U.S. government representatives announced that four people, including two Russian intelligence officers, were charged with stealing military secrets, money, and hundreds of millions of Yahoo! email accounts. It was the largest data breach up to that time.

QUESTIONS TO ASK

Within this book are three types of boxes with questions to help your critical thinking about digital data security. The icons will help you identify them.

THE CENTRAL ISSUES
Learning about the main points of information.

WHAT'S AT STAKE
Helping you determine how the issue will affect you.

ASK YOUR OWN QUESTIONS
Prompts to address gaps in your understanding.

STAYING SAFE

Digital data security is a major issue that is growing, affecting people globally. Banks store and share financial information, health care centers store medical records, and schools keep digital files of students' grades and other personal details. You and your friends may share information and interact with one another and the outside world on **social media** and via online games and user groups.

Hackers try to find weak links in **software**, **hardware**, and processes that they can use to gain access to private information. Digital data security refers to various ways to stop them from gaining access to this. Passwords, **backups**, **firewalls**, and data **encryption** programs are examples of data security measures.

ON THE RISE

As more people use computers, the risk of falling **victim** to a cybercrime increases greatly. In the United States, cybercrime is the fastest-growing criminal activity. Each year, tens of millions of digital records are exposed across the nation. In fact, there is a hacker attack every 39 seconds, and cybercrimes make up half of all crimes in the entire world. People and industries lose more than $100 billion each year in this way.

Cybercrimes—those related to computers— are much like traditional crimes. Some hackers look for personal information and credit card numbers that they can use to steal your identity and buy things with your money. Others work for governments, stealing military details.

Surveys show that while 80 percent of U.S. citizens believe cybersecurity is important, only 56 percent have taken active measures to protect themselves from cybercrimes. Computer experts predict that by 2020 there will be more than 200 billion connected devices, so it is essential for everyone to know the facts about digital data security. If you use a computer or use any services that store your information on a computer, you need to know what it is and why it matters.

The best way to protect against becoming a victim of cybercrime is to get informed about digital data security and how you can protect your computer and your online activity. The key to this is understanding the types of crimes that take place and how cybercriminals target individuals and businesses.

UNDERSTANDING THE ISSUE

Start by learning about the background of digital data security. This will help you understand the **context** and build a vocabulary of key terms. Make sure you look for different **perspectives** on the issue, from those of hackers to major corporations and governments to victims. This will help you develop a well-balanced viewpoint so you can make informed decisions about cybersecurity and how best to protect yourself.

Once informed about the issue, you need to stay up to date. Ensure you always have the latest details since facts and theories change over time. Cybercriminals are always finding new ways to access information. Also, data security experts are constantly coming up with new software and procedures to help you stay safe. Being informed will help you understand the wider world and how global events impact your life.

▲ Smartphones are full of digital data, including personal details and phone, bank, and health records, which hackers can access and use.

THE CENTRAL ISSUES

Cybercrimes often go unnoticed or unreported. Why may this be a problem for individuals, businesses, and governments? How do you think cybercrimes could affect you, your family, friends, and your community?

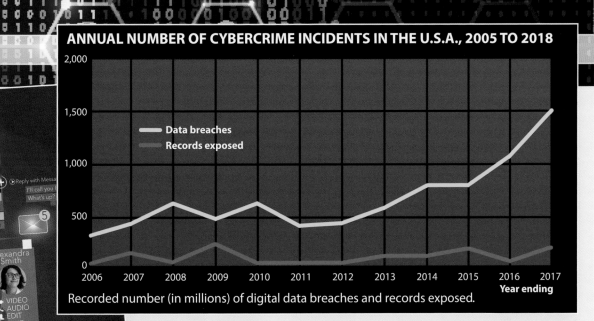

ANNUAL NUMBER OF CYBERCRIME INCIDENTS IN THE U.S.A., 2005 TO 2018

Data breaches
Records exposed

Year ending

Recorded number (in millions) of digital data breaches and records exposed.

> *As the world is increasingly interconnected, everyone shares the responsibility of securing cyberspace.* From computer scientist Newton Lee's 2013 book, *Counterterrorism and Cybersecurity: Total Information Awareness*

▼ On June 25, 2015, millions of U.S. government employees and job applicants had their data stolen during a computer breach. Officials reported the incident to the Senate Homeland Security and Governmental Affairs Committee.

To fully understand the importance of digital data security and how to achieve it, you need context for the issue. Context is the background, setting, or circumstances for an event, idea, or situation. It helps you understand how an issue came to be and its impact. For example, to understand why companies, governments, and other organizations are making huge investments in digital data security, you should learn about cybercrimes and their impact on **society**.

KEY TERMS

Hacking refers to gaining unauthorized access into a computer system or network.

Malware is a type of software that damages or disables a computer system.

Ransomware is a type of malware that shuts down a computer system until the victim pays a ransom.

Bugs are errors in software that cause it not to work properly.

Viruses are software programs that spread from one computer to another—often through email—and cause damage by deleting files or corrupting data.

Phishing is a type of **fraud** that aims to gain sensitive information through fake emails and texts.

Mr. Mark Zuckerberg

▼ Facebook founder Mark Zuckerberg was forced to answer questions before the U.S. Congress in April 2018 after the company revealed major privacy breaches. Facebook admitted the private data of 87 million Facebook users was accessed through a quiz app and that most of its 2.2 billion users have had their public profiles scraped for information by scam artists or identity thieves. Congress was interested in increasing regulations to protect data security and privacy.

WHERE TO START

To build up the context, you must research and investigate thoroughly. The Internet is a good place to start looking for information. Using the Internet, you can tap into newspapers and journals from around the world. You can watch videos, listen to podcasts, read blog posts, and much more. You can use a search engine to look for general information, or you can access directories and online databases dedicated to a particular subject.

Not all information is, or need be, online. Libraries and archives are other good sources of background information. They have a variety of printed materials that you may not be able to access anywhere else, such as historic newspaper articles, images, audio recordings, and government reports. Librarians can help you search for information and offer advice about where to look to find reliable, top-quality material.

FORMING A PICTURE

The more you learn about digital data security, the easier it will be to make sense of new information about the issue. Learning its history from various perspectives will help you learn about key concepts and important people and events that have shaped it. Reading newspaper articles and watching daily TV news will give you an insight into what is happening today.

Because there is so much information available on the subject, it can be a challenge to build up a complete picture. But there are some basic research guidelines you can follow.

Publications, videos, websites, and other types of information are source materials. Primary source materials are firsthand accounts of a topic. They are original materials written, recorded, or created by people who had a direct connection to the subject. A report written by a computer engineer about a digital data breach is an example of a primary source. Other examples of primary sources include personal diaries, survey results, government documents, handwritten notes, photographs, and speeches.

Secondary sources are **interpretations** of a topic created by people who did not have direct experience of the event or situation. They are often made by **summarizing** information found in primary sources. A chart showing **statistics** from various sources about different types of cybercrimes is an example of a secondary source. Biographies, encyclopedias, textbooks, and journal articles are other examples.

Tertiary sources provide information about where to find primary and secondary sources. Bibliographies, directories, and indexes are examples of tertiary sources. They guide you to other sources you can use to learn more about a topic.

FINDING QUALITY SOURCES

Not all sources are created equal. Some provide more reliable information than others. How can you tell if a source is **credible**? Ask yourself the following questions:

- Does the creator have experience, skills, or education related to the topic?
- When was the source created? Facts and information are always changing.
- Is the source well written? Does it have errors? Does it include a list of sources to back up facts?
- What is the purpose of the source? Does it project a specific point of view?
- Who is the target audience? Is it meant to appeal to a certain group of people?

If the creator is not an expert, or the source is very old, badly written, or doesn't have a balanced view, look elsewhere for your main information.

EHR system

HN xxxx-xxxx

AGE xxxxx
GENDER xxxxx
WEIGHT xxxxx
HEIGHT xxxxx
BMI xxxxx
FAT xxxxx

DIAGNOSIS

▶ Patients' health information can be stored and displayed on devices such as tablet computers. It is important that these devices have security measures such as passwords and firewalls.

VISUAL MATERIALS

Sometimes, information is presented in the form of a visual such as a chart, table, map, or graph (see page 7). These graphic formats are often used to organize and summarize information in a way that is more meaningful and easier to remember. Data, statistics, and figures work well in a visual format. For example, statistics about the types of cyberattacks can be shown in a pie chart (see page 39). This helps us compare different attacks and make conclusions about which are most common.

FREE **LONDON WEDNESDAY 21**

Evening Standa

WE HAVE OUR STRUGG

LIAM PAYNE ON HIS RELATIONSHIP WITH CHERYL ›› EXCLUSIVE INTERVI

PLUS: PAYBACK TIME FOR LONDON'S YOUNG BUYERS ›› HOMES &

FACEBOOK DATA GRAB 'IS JUST TIP OF ICEBERG'

SHOCK CLAIM FROM ACADEMIC WHO SAYS: I'M THE
L GUY OVER HARVESTING OF PRIVATE DETAILS

**Joe Murphy and
Nicholas Cecil**

THE Facebook data scandal deepened today as a Cambridge academic who harvested 30 million people's private details from the site said "tens of thousands" of other apps had done th

stocks to tumble by tens of millions of pounds,
Dr Kogan said he had not known that the personal information he obtained from Facebook users by paying them to take a "personality test" might be used f

Happy landing: Andria Za husband John and d

▲ Cybercrime is global. By 2017, about one fourth of all companies worldwide had experienced a data breach.

INSURANCE
SCHEDULE

APPOINTMENT
HEALTH PLAN

INFORMATION
HEALTH STATUS

PERSONAL HEALTH RECORD

BLOOD PRESSURE
SYSTOLIC
DIASTOLIC

BLOOD SUGAR TESTS
GLUCOSE
HbA1C

PLASMA
HEMOGLOBIN

Examination   Radiology   Laboratory

MEDICAL HISTORY — NURSE NOTE — PHARMACY

TMENT

Previous   Done   Next   Exit

> **"** *The way that people think about privacy is changing a bit...What people want isn't complete privacy. It isn't that they want secrecy. It's that they want control over what they share and what they don't.* **"**
>
> Facebook CEO Mark Zuckerberg in a *Time* magazine article in 2010

It is important to use a variety of sources to ensure you have a balanced view of a topic. By learning something from each source, you will achieve the best results. Sets of facts and figures will often be interpreted differently by people of opposing opinions and perspectives. Allowing for this is especially important when looking for ways to solve a problem such as fixing a weakness in a company's digital data security. It is a good idea to consider perspectives on a topic that are different from your own.

When people share the same perspectives, they may miss out on new opportunities and solutions. For example, a group of in-house software experts may agree their company needs to purchase new security software to reduce cyberthreats. An independent expert may say a better and cheaper solution is to train staff to use existing security measures more effectively.

MOST IMPORTANT ONLINE SAFETY TOPICS IN THE U.S.A., JUNE 2016

- Preventing identity theft
- Keeping my devices secure
- How to identify fake messages
- How to tell if a website is secure
- How to report online security problems
- How young people are lured online
- How to manage my online privacy
- Dealing with online bullying
- Blocking people online
- Risks of sexting

online teens
parents of online teens

0%   10%   20%   30%   40%   50%   60%

Views of 804 online teens and 810 parents of online teens

CONSIDERING BIAS

Each source of information contains bias. Bias is a prejudice for or against someone or something. Be cautious of bias when **evaluating** source materials. Use the following tips to identify bias in a source:

- Does the source present various points of view?
- Will the source gain anything by expressing a certain point of view?
- Was the source created for a specific purpose?
- Does the source use extreme language to create positive or negative impressions?

A BALANCED VIEW

Bias can be accidental or deliberate. For each source, you need to determine which bias it is. However, when you use a range of reliable sources, bias becomes more balanced. With digital data security, you need to consider the views of computer manufacturers, software developers, cybersecurity experts, computer users, Internet service providers—and even the perspective of cybercriminals. Some cybercriminals believe they are exposing the wrongdoing of corporations and governments (see page 22).

▲ An antivirus software survey showed that only 61 percent of young people actively use the privacy settings on social media sites. Yet 83 percent said they were worried about their privacy.

▼ Ninety-five percent of U.S. teens have access to a smartphone, which can be hacked. Digital data security is an issue for these devices in the same way it is for a desktop or network computer.

Digital data security involves protecting computers from a breach. Breaches happen when a person or company gains unauthorized access to view, share, or use sensitive, confidential, or protected information. Personal information, such as social security and credit card numbers as well as medical histories, is often the target of data breaches. Many people are targeted by cybercriminals and do not even realize it. However, **identity theft** is just one potential negative consequence of a data breach.

▶ A cybersecurity officer runs diagnostics, or checks on information systems, at a company's computer database. Companies regularly test their digital data security systems to ensure they cannot be breached.

USEFUL DATA AND INFORMATION

"Data" is any collection of numbers, words, images, sounds, and computer coding. "Information" includes reports, articles, medical records, and personal files. Common computer breaches often involve business information such as details about products that are in development, client lists, and financial records. If this information falls into the wrong hands, it can be used to cause major problems for a company. For example, competitor companies can use the confidential data to create their own software, and the information to steal clients and improve their own products.

TYPES OF BREACHES

Most data breaches take place online or across computer networks. Many are intentional. They happen when a person purposely tries to gain access to information they should not have so they can use it either for personal gain or to sabotage another person or company.

Some data breaches are unintentional. In fact, studies show that more than 40 percent of data breaches that take place within companies are the result of employees', or workers', **negligence**. Employees share their passwords, leave their computers unlocked, or walk away from their desks with sensitive information displayed on their computer screen for anyone to see.

Cybercriminals use many methods and tools to commit crimes. Malware and social engineering scams are just a few examples (see Breach Facts panel).

BREACH FACTS

Social engineering involves tricking people into providing confidential data. Hackers often use it to learn people's passwords or gain access to their accounts. They may send emails or texts pretending to be a trusted source such as a well-known company. These emails often contain links the user must click to verify their information. They may also include an attachment that, if downloaded, installs malware onto the user's device.

15

The Internet exists as an invisible network. In seeming to connect everyone, it gives people a false sense of both security and **anonymity**. Surely, if information and computer service providers are taking steps to avoid data breaches, you don't need your own security measures? Wrong. Believing everyone is anonymous leads some people to lose their **inhibitions** and take part in online crimes they would not be comfortable committing in person.

Even people who are not hackers may illegally download information, such as movies, music, or books, thinking their actions will go unnoticed or without realizing they are committing a crime. But on the Internet, almost every computer can be identified and often its location is known as well.

UNAWARE OF THE ISSUE

There is no law stating companies have to tell people when they have experienced a data breach, but word of the breach often gets out one way or another. Either an incident occurs that people start to question, or the hacker or someone who suspects a hack makes a public claim, or the company that has been hacked simply comes forward and lets people know what happened.

Looking at the history of computers and digital data security will help you better understand the threats and impact of cybercrime and the importance of the issue today.

When the Internet first became public in the 1990s, people were naïve to the threats they could face as they connected to networks. Many believed breaches that occurred at major organizations, such as health care or financial centers, would remain at the source so they did not need to worry about them personally.

WHAT'S AT STAKE?

People often believe their actions over the Internet are harmless or go unseen because they are inside a "bubble" and not in the real world. Do you think stealing a person's identity or financial information to use for personal gain is a serious crime? Is downloading music illegally worse than hacking into a corporate database?

▶ In 1989, British computer scientist Sir Tim Berners-Lee found a way to make the Internet open to the general public. To highlight the worldwide web of digital data, he displayed the message "This is for everyone" at the opening ceremony of the 2012 Olympics in London. Billions of people watched the event live.

AN IMPENDING THREAT

Over time and through bad experiences, individuals learned the importance of digital data security. Governments, schools, law enforcement agencies, businesses, and other organizations began to realize they needed to take more responsibility when it came to providing guidance about how to protect against unwanted intrusions. Gradually though, hackers and cybercriminals found ways to overcome security measures and realized the many ways they could exploit the data and information they accessed.

▲ Home computers first became popular in the 1980s. At that time, before the Internet, "digital data security," "cybercrime," and "hackers" were not everyday terms and they hardly impacted personal computer users. All that would change, in a major way.

Digital security threats date back to the beginning of computers and the Internet. The concept of computers developed in the 1930s, and they were used at government and academic institutions in the 1940s and 1950s. Soon, people began storing data on computers such as research studies and reports. At first, the biggest threats to digital data were simply people working inside these institutions who were able to open and read confidential files that did not belong to them.

Throughout the 1960s, people looked for ways to allow computers to share information. At the time, information could be stored only on separate computers. It could not be viewed on another computer without being physically embedded on that machine. There was no data transfer technology linking machines.

On national and international levels, government and academic organizations wanted to share and exchange information within and between their computer systems. This would allow researchers, scientists, planners, directors, and others to quickly and easily learn from one another and share ideas without the need to use the same computers or send information in hard copy, such as printed documents.

THE COLD WAR

In the 1950s and 1960s, during the height of the Cold War between the United States and the **Soviet Union**, the U.S. government feared the Soviets would attack the country's communications systems. Back then, there were only a few computer systems across the country, and each worked in **isolation**. If any system went down, it could be disastrous, as the information on that computer potentially would be lost or

▶ Early attempts to provide the general public with free access to gaming, banking, and online media services did not foresee, or overlooked, the potential problems of digital data security. Today, despite sophisticated cybersecurity, computer systems can be breached.

▶ Early computer systems rarely used passwords. Today, about 40 percent of U.S. citizens have shared their online passwords with friends or family. They also use the same password for many of their accounts. Even with security measures in place, hackers can easily access digital data.

difficult to retrieve. The U.S. government wanted to develop a reliable communications network that would continue to function even if several systems collapsed.

INVENTING ARPANET

The Advanced Research Projects Agency (ARPA), a government-funded initiative, began working with computer scientists at several top-ranked universities across the country to build a computer network. In 1969, the agency founded ARPANET. It connected four university computers on the same network so they could share resources and information, and communicate between institutions.

ASK YOUR OWN QUESTIONS

Consider the different communications systems available to you, including those that are not digital. Are all of them open to security breaches? Which do you feel is the safest? On what basis? Which is the least safe? Why?

ARPANET became the basis for the Internet as we know it today. At the time, it had no obvious security controls—no computer checkpoints, police, or regulators—to help prevent cybersecurity issues. No one thought there was a need for them. It was up to the people who used the system to protect themselves and govern their own online activity.

Few of the people who built ARPANET thought it would become so popular or widely available. They realized its potential but did not put a lot of thought into how it could be used for negative purposes or the ways it could be breached, hacked into, and disrupted. In fact, in the early days of ARPANET, there were few threats that even came to mind, so its inventors focused more on getting the system to work than its potential risks.

▼ Anonymous is a group of hackers who are best known for their protests and online attacks against governments, agencies, and organizations that they believe are censoring or controlling information. They released a statement explaining who they are and how they choose their targets.

THE FIRST VIRUS AND ANTIVIRUS

Soon after ARPANET was developed, the first cybercrime took place. In 1971, the Creeper virus was released. It moved between computers that were connected on the same network. The objective of the virus was not to damage computers but to show how quickly a threat could **mobilize**. Instead of destroying files or corrupting infected computers, a message popped up on-screen. It said, *"I'm the Creeper, catch me if you can."* Creeper proved a program could move from one computer to another without human help.

Two years after Creeper made its first appearance, the world's first antivirus software was made. Reaper, as it was known, removed Creeper from computer systems. No one knows for sure who developed the software. Some people believe it was the same man who developed Creeper, Bob Thomas, in an effort to control its spread.

KEY PLAYERS

J. C. R. Licklider was a computer scientist whose early ideas about computer time-sharing and human–computer interactions led to the development of ARPANET. Licklider wrote a series of memos about his idea for an "Intergalactic Computer Network." After taking a job as a director at ARPA, he began sharing his thoughts on computer networking with his peers and laying the groundwork for the Internet today.

Hackers are people with excellent computer skills—see the Key Players panel. They often create and alter computer programs, pushing the boundaries of what technology can do. In the 1960s, Massachusetts Institute of Technology (MIT) students began tinkering with computer code to find new ways of processing and handling data to make computers work better and faster. These students became the world's first hackers.

As computers became more popular, some hackers would break into computer systems simply to take look around or fix bugs. Others discovered they could **manipulate** systems for their own personal gain. Over time, governments, military agencies, and businesses began to realize they could use hackers to learn one another's secrets by breaking into computer systems. Many organizations began to employ hackers to do this type of work, which led to identity theft, fraud, professional **espionage**, and international crimes.

INTERNET EXPLOSION

By the time the Internet was available to the public in 1991, cybersecurity was already a growing concern. Browser add-ons and software programs such as Flash and music players left Internet users open to vulnerabilities. These programs were riddled with bugs, viruses, and worms.

By 1996, phishing scams had become a reality, and within the next few years adware and spyware began to gain popularity. When smartphones then hit the market, people became even more vulnerable to cybersecurity threats. Companies quickly began to ramp up their digital data security systems. Some even started to hire "white hat" hackers to help them stay on top of their game and one step ahead of "black hat" hackers.

KEY PLAYERS

White hat, or ethical, hackers are computer security specialists. They have permission to break into computer networks and databases to help people and companies find flaws in their systems. They look for ways to repair weaknesses and protect systems from attack.

Black hat, or unethical, hackers are people who look for vulnerabilities in systems and use them for personal gain. They enter computer systems without permission. They may spread viruses, send phishing emails, or use other means to steal data with **malicious** intent.

Gray hat hackers do not have authorization to enter a system like white hat hackers but they also do not have malicious intent like black hat hackers. They often use their skills to explore systems and may even fix the issues they find.

▼ In May 2017, many thousands of computers across the world were attacked by WannaCry ransomware. The cryptoworm attacked computers running the Microsoft Windows operating system. Users were asked for payments in **bitcoins** to avoid having their data disrupted. Within days, Microsoft killed off the attack, but damage ran into billions of dollars.

MAJOR TACTICS USED BY CYBERCRIMINALS IN NORTH AMERICA

Breaches involving stolen and/or weak passwords	**81%**
Breaches involving hacking software	**62%**
Breaches involving malware	**51%**
Social media attacks	**43%**
Exploiting user errors	**14%**
Physical actions	**8%**

Many breaches involve more than one tactic.
Based on 50,000+ cybercrimes in 2017.

English

Ooops, your files have been encrypted!

What Happened to My Computer?

Your important files are encrypted.
Many of your documents, photos, videos, databases an[d]
accessible because they have been encrypted. Maybe y[ou]
recover your files, but do not waste your time. Nobod[y]
our decryption service.

Can I Recover My Files?

e raised on

01:42

ft

4:28

@WanaDecryptor@

You did not pay or we did not confirmed your payment!
Pay now if you didn't and check again after 2 hours.

Best time to check: 9:00am - 11:00am GMT from Monday to Friday

OK

I be lost on

6:01:42

eft

4:28

Please check the current price of Bitcoin and buy so[me]
click <How to buy bitcoins>.
And send the correct amount to the address specified in this window.
After your payment, click <Check Payment>. Best time to check: 9:00am

Bitcoin.com

BUY BITCOINS!
Touch the screen to start

bitcoin ATH

▲ A bitcoin digital currency machine in Hong Kong, China. More than $1.1 billion in bitcoin was stolen by hackers in the first half of 2018 alone.

4 AN INFORMED DECISION

There is no shortage of information in the world. From newspapers and podcasts to websites and streaming videos, accessing information has never been easier. However, not all of the information is accurate. Anyone can post anything online and, in many cases, no one has checked that the facts are correct and free of bias. As a result, **myths**, lies, and misinformation spread quickly from one source to another.

Scotiabank

Inclusion makes us stronger

We celebrate all the possibilities of you

Scotiabank

24/7 banking at your convenience

NO LOITERING

ASK YOUR OWN QUESTIONS

Why is it important to develop information literacy skills? What can happen if people believe all the information they come across without evaluating it first?

▼ Hackers are always finding new ways to steal money from automated teller machine (ATM) users. Financial institutions, such as Scotiabank, use strong security measures to protect against attacks. A Personal Identification Number (PIN) works like a password to help keep your account information secure.

TAKING CARE

Social engineering attacks, especially those involving the use of phishing or malware, rely on the fact that many people believe what they read. For example, you may receive an email from a long-lost relative in another country who wants to send you money. All you need to do is click a link to deposit the funds in your bank. It may seem too good to be true because it likely is.

To become an informed citizen, you have a responsibility to make sure any information you access is credible and reliable. You need to fact-check your sources and find **evidence** that supports the opinions people share with you through social media and conversations.

INFORMATION LITERACY

Studying a range of relevant source materials and then sorting and evaluating the information they contain is known as information literacy. Developing these skills involves being able to:

- recognize the quality and importance of information so you can select and prioritize which to rely on the most
- evaluate information critically and competently. For example, a company selling cybersecurity software may provide biased information to promote its products, or a **chief evangelist** at a software company may be better at explaining the benefits of a software program than another staff member
- apply the information in a way that will help you make decisions or conclusions.

> " *One of the main cyber-risks is to think they don't exist. The other is to try to treat all potential risks.* "
>
> Stéphane Nappo, Global Chief Information Security Officer at Société Générale International Banking

THE CENTRAL ISSUES

What do cyberattacks like those on Facebook in 2018 (see page 35) tell us about our own digital data security? Why must everyone protect themselves from hackers? What may happen if they do not? Who should be responsible for preventing global cybercrime—governments, Internet service providers, or social media companies?

▶ Via satellites, communication centers, and underground and undersea cables, every country in the world is interconnected. To keep this network safe, experts believe there will be more than 3.5 million cybersecurity job openings globally by 2021.

There are many different perspectives on how digital data security impacts people and businesses, and whose responsibility it is to help protect against cyberthreats. You should consider a variety of these before you form an opinion of your own about the issues.

PRIVATE CITIZENS

Many individuals and small companies believe they do not have any information worth stealing and so do not have sophisticated digital data security measures. They believe big businesses are the main targets of cybercrime. However, private citizens and family-run stores are just as much at risk as large organizations and government offices. The Internet and other computer networks tie people together in all parts of the world. This means someone in Vietnam could access digital data from someone in Canada and vice versa. Security threats are not bound by physical walls or country borders.

BASIC PRECAUTIONS

Surveys show that 64 percent of U.S. citizens have personally experienced the impact of data theft, and nearly half feel their personal data is more at risk today than it was five years ago. Credit card fraud is one of the most common concerns, and 41 percent of card owners have been charged for purchases they did not make. Another 35 percent have had account information and other details compromised. Many others have had their email or social media accounts hacked.

While more and more people are becoming aware of cyberthreats, many people still do not take the appropriate measures to protect themselves. According to a Pew Research Center study, nearly 70 percent of adult computer and smartphone users in North America are not concerned about making sure their digital passwords are secure. Even those who have experienced a cybersecurity issue do not take any extra password precautions.

◄ Internet banking is a key target for cybercrime. In May 2018, Canada's Bank of Montreal and CIBC Simplii Financial online bank reported a data breach involving tens of thousands of customers. The hackers demanded $1 million in cryptocurrency or they would release the account details.

When it comes to protecting their secrets, many large companies will stop at nothing. They have thousands of employees, each with multiple computer devices that are connected to the company network. A breach of any one of these devices could spell disaster for the company. The last thing they want is for their competition to get their hands on trade secrets or for criminals to ruin their reputation by stealing client information.

TAKING THREATS SERIOUSLY

Many big businesses use employee awareness **campaigns** to ensure their staff understands the various threats they may encounter each day and how to respond to those threats in a **proactive** way. This may involve teaching them how to identify phishing emails or other social engineering scams. Companies often also have strict digital data security **policies** that all employees must follow under threat of losing their job if they do not. These policies include specific details about using passwords to protect devices, online accounts, and software programs.

▼ A trader in company shares looks at financial data from markets around the world. Experts estimate the volume of data output will increase at least four times by 2020 and that more than 30 percent of all data will live in or pass through the computer **cloud**.

▶ Hackers developing online security software. Money gained by cybercrimes in 2018 is expected to top $1.5 trillion. More than half will come from online markets.

STAFF RESPONSIBILITY

Companies that have digital data policies make their employees responsible for keeping the highest possible security standards in order to help protect the company. This includes telling staff not to download software due to potential viruses and/or not to use company devices for personal projects, business, or social media, exposing the company to fraud or ransom. Many businesses even hire ethical hackers (see page 22) to help secure their systems from cyberattacks.

LIMITED RESOURCES

Small and medium-sized businesses often spend more time focusing on their customers than their digital data security measures. A recent survey of these businesses in Canada showed that as many as 70 percent have no data **protocols** in place. Many do not have the resources— money, staff, or modern computers and software—to establish a digital security system. They often fail to see the risk or the impact a breach could have on their company, thinking they are too small for a hacker to notice.

KEY PLAYERS

Australian cybersecurity expert **Chris Rock** is a white hat hacker who is known for exposing major threats in a big way. In 2015, Rock showed attendees at DEF CON, one of the world's biggest hacking conferences, just how easy it was to hack into a hospital database to issue death certificates instead of discharge notices for living people. The certificates could then be used to collect life insurance policies, for example.

The following year, Rock explained how easily hackers can overthrow a government by using their skills to secure weapons and financing. Rock is always researching vulnerabilities and reporting his findings.

TRUST ISSUES

Studies suggest half of the U.S. population believe their data is not as secure today as it was five years ago. They do not trust people and organizations that are meant to take steps to prevent cybercrime. Massive breaches involving big, well-known, and respected businesses around the world have only fueled this fire. For example, taxi company Uber tried to cover up an attack that occurred in October 2016 that put confidential data, such as names, email addresses, and phone numbers, of more than 57 million users into the hands of hackers. The company allegedly paid the people responsible for the breach $100,000 to delete the data and keep quiet about the incident.

CYBERCRIME AS MAJOR FEAR OF U.S. CITIZENS, 2017

% of adults who said they frequently or occasionally feared being a victim of:

%	Category
67	Cybercrime
66	Victim of identity theft
38	Car stolen or broken into
36	Home burglarized when you are not there
30	Victim of terrorism
26	Your child harmed at school
25	Getting mugged
23	Home burglarized when you are there
22	Hate crime
18	Getting murdered

Based on a poll of 1,028 citizens aged 18+ in October 2017

◄ Mobile malware can be used to hack into iPhones, car communication systems, and other devices. Users are typically tricked into downloading software that lets hackers steal personal information, photographs, and chat messages.

MEGA INCIDENTS

The following year, the public learned Deep Root Analytics, a company hired by the Republican Party to gather information about U.S. voters during the 2016 campaign, accidentally leaked the private details of nearly 200 million people. Their information had been stored on the cloud without any form of password protection for two weeks before the incident occurred.

In September 2017, Equifax, a major credit reporting agency, announced a cyberattack had exposed the personal information of more than 143 million people earlier that year. The hackers were able to gain access to salary and tax information.

RESPONSIBILITIES

People want reassurance that their personal information is protected from threats while working online. They want to know the details of their private lives are not being shared with anyone they do not want to have them. This information includes health records, family and friends' addresses and phone numbers, driver's license and passport details, and credit card numbers. Customers hold the businesses that require this information accountable for maintaining the highest possible security standards. However, everyone is responsible for their own digital data security, and they must take appropriate precautions to protect themselves from breaches too.

◄ Between 2005 and 2007, a massive breach of credit card data took place. Albert Gonzalez led a team that stole information from about 45.7 million TJX payment cards, costing the company around $256 million. The incident opened many companies' eyes to the very real threat of cybercrimes.

31

Governments are among the most vulnerable organizations when it comes to digital data security. Cyberattacks can have a devastating impact on national services and homeland security.

CRIME AT THE HIGHEST LEVEL

In February 2017, in Bingham County, Idaho, hackers used ransomware to attack multiple systems and force the county to pay a ransom to recover their information. That same year, WannaCry ransomware (see page 23) hit government departments worldwide in countries such as the U.K., Russia, China, and Romania.

Between 2013 and 2015, the government of Canada was the target of about 2,500 state-sponsored cyberattacks per year. At least one attack was successful in breaching government systems each week. In 2014, the personnel management of the U.S. government was breached. The records of about 18 million people were hacked as a result.

PRIME TARGETS

Governments are vulnerable because they employ many people, any one of whom may accidentally—or deliberately—not follow the digital data security guidelines. Being large organizations, they are unable to change computer systems and work practices quickly. **Complacency**, failure to share information between departments, and often old software and hardware are other factors making hacking likely.

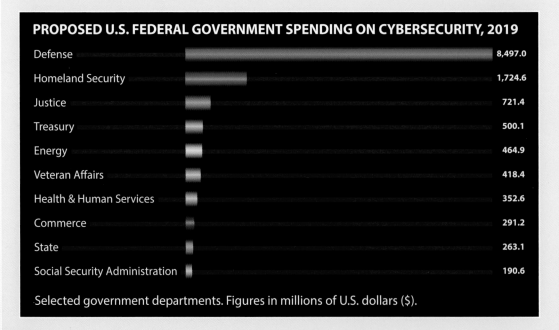

PROPOSED U.S. FEDERAL GOVERNMENT SPENDING ON CYBERSECURITY, 2019

Department	Amount
Defense	8,497.0
Homeland Security	1,724.6
Justice	721.4
Treasury	500.1
Energy	464.9
Veteran Affairs	418.4
Health & Human Services	352.6
Commerce	291.2
State	263.1
Social Security Administration	190.6

Selected government departments. Figures in millions of U.S. dollars ($).

SETTING STANDARDS

In 2018, the U.S. Department of Homeland Security announced that Russian government hackers had gained access to the control rooms of power plants across the country over the past year. While there is no evidence the Russians took over the plants, the potential for them to do so was real. The hackers could have shut down power across the country, switching off everything from water treatment to sewage systems and refrigeration.

To try to combat similar breaches, the U.S. Federal Trade Commission (FTC) issues regular guidelines and reports on successful actions against cybercrimes. In Europe, the General Data Protection Regulation (GDPR) has been rolled out. It aims to create consistent data privacy requirements across the 28 member countries.

▼ Cybercrime is the most recent issue addressed by the 10 countries of the Association of Southeast Asian Nations (ASEAN).

KEY PLAYERS

The **National Security Agency** (NSA) is a U.S. intelligence section of the Department of Defense. One of its roles is to constantly watch for cyberthreats and introduce defense and security measures to stop government computer systems from being breached. It trains computer experts and works with foreign intelligence services to minimize, intercept, and overcome cybercrime.

In Canada, a similar cybersurveillance and defense system is run by the Canadian Security Intelligence Service (CSIS).

5TH ASEAN DEFENCE MINISTERS' MEETING–PLUS
Strengthening Cooperation, Building Resilience

20 OCTOBER 2018
SINGAPORE

▲ LinkedIn is an online business community. In one breach, cybercriminals hacked into certain LinkedIn accounts and sent private messages to other LinkedIn users. The messages included a link that redirected people to a phishing website.

▼ Cyberstalking, which includes cyberbullying and online harassment, is one of the most common cybercrimes among teens. Social media is commonly used to carry out these behaviors. Approximately 8 percent of North Americans have experienced fear and felt unsafe due to cyberstalking.

Sharing information with friends and family around the world is one of the biggest benefits of social networking. Billions of people use social media platforms each day, but there are some risks that come with using these sites. Even when the highest security settings are applied, it is still possible for hackers to break into an account. Many major social media platforms have been hacked and had data stolen from millions of accounts.

ALL DATA IS VALUABLE

In 2018, Facebook announced that a weak link in the platform's code left at least 50 million Facebook accounts open to an attack in September of that year. Hackers found a weakness in the platform that would allow them to take over the at-risk accounts and gain access to private data.

Social media posts often contain private information hackers can use to learn more about a person. For example, "What is your pet's name?" is a common answer to security questions for recovering a password. People sometimes post pictures of their pets along with its name, which hackers can then use to break into private accounts. For this reason, it is important to be careful about the information you post online.

SECURITY SETTINGS

Privacy controls on social media sites limit how much information is accessible to others. However, locking down an account too much could defeat the purpose of having the account at all, since no one will be able to see the posts. It is important to strike a balance between what you share freely and what you keep secure. Look for privacy-setting options on the sites and search engines you use.

WHAT'S AT STAKE?

If social media companies repeatedly fail to keep people's online details safe, should governments step in and close them down? What might be the impact on society if social media companies were shut down?

▼ Many people spend more than 35 minutes a day on Facebook.

5 STAYING INFORMED

Our knowledge of digital data security threats and protective measures is constantly changing and expanding. Hackers are finding new ways to break through cybersecurity measures. In response, people and organizations are regularly assessing and changing the systems and policies they have in place to prevent breaches. It used to be that a computer password could be just three letters. Today, most companies require a minimum string of eight letters, numbers, or symbols so the password is harder for hackers to crack.

THE CENTRAL ISSUES

Should we consider the perspective of hackers who commit cybercrimes (see page 22)? For instance, why do white hat hackers choose to use their skills to benefit others when they could potentially make more money as black hat hackers? What do gray hat hackers hope to achieve by exposing breaches to the world?

▼ Though most newspapers try to represent many views, some use biased or emotional language to push one perspective. Some newspapers have criticized U.S. president Donald Trump's friendly relationship with Russian president Vladimir Putin, in large part because of the Russian government hacks on the 2016 presidential election (see bottom right).

GOOD SOURCES

We learn from events that happened in the past so we can avoid the same mistakes in the future. For this reason, not only must you get informed—you must also stay informed. Watching the news, reading blogs, listening to podcasts, and talking to people with a variety of opinions are all good ways to stay informed and gain a balanced perspective. Some good, specific source materials about digital data security and cybercrimes can be found by:

- reading blogs and online news sources such as *Krebs on Security, Threat Level, Security Weekly, The Hacker News,* and *Dark Reading*
- talking to IT and network specialists who deal with cyberthreats regularly
- following experts, such as Brian Krebs and Bruce Schneier, on social media sites
- listening to podcasts such as *The CyberWire, EuroTrash,* and *Sans Internet Storm Center*
- signing up for alerts and advisories such as CERT/CC, ICS-CERT, and SecurityFocus.

◄ In fall 2015, the Federal Bureau of Investigation (FBI) learned that Russian hackers had breached the Democratic Party's computer network, possibly to damage the reputation of Democratic presidential candidate Hillary Clinton. She lost the 2016 election to Donald Trump.

Organizations of all sizes and categories are increasingly coming under cyberattack. Some of the threats are short-lived and easily overcome. Others are long-term and widespread. For example, in March 2018, the United States arrested nine Iranian government hackers who had stolen large amounts of data from 144 U.S. universities and 176 universities in 21 other countries since 2013.

FUTURE TRENDS

One new trend for stopping cyberattacks is based on **machine learning**—a type of software that can change and adapt when it receives new information. It can be used to automatically identify cyberattacks and defend against them. Anti-spam software is a good example. It has the ability to identify new types of junk mail over time.

Machine learning can also be used to stop Distributed Denial of Service (DDoS) attacks. Hackers use a network of computers infected with malware, or botnets, to attack a website. They send so much spam and so many data requests to the site that it overloads and crashes. DDoS detection software uses machine learning to find out from user and data patterns within a network which requests are fake and prevent them from reaching their targets.

Cloud ransomware targets photos, music, and all types of documents on the cloud. Massive cloud services, such as Google, Amazon, and IBM, are well prepared to handle hacker attacks but smaller services may not have the experience and finances to ward off threats.

Fileless attacks use software that is already installed on a computer to attack the system. Hackers use weaknesses in the software to get inside the system. As a result, fileless attacks often go undetected by antivirus software.

▼ Electricity-generating plants are among the 60 percent of organizations that believe **Internet of Things** (IoT) devices are a high risk for ransomware attacks, and 97 percent say an attack would devastate their business.

> " Everybody should want to make sure that we have the cyber tools necessary to investigate cyber crimes, and to be prepared to defend against them and to bring people to justice who commit it. "
>
> Janet Reno, former attorney general of the United States

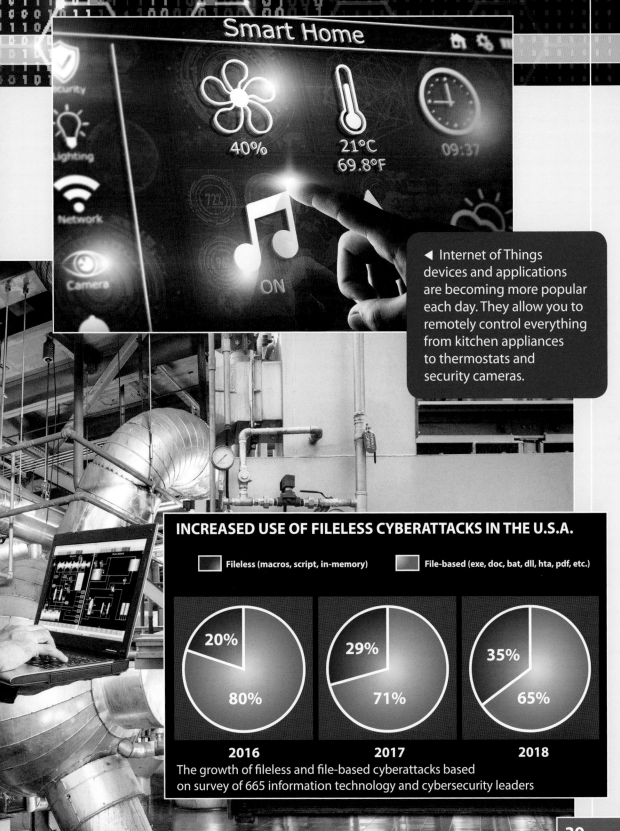

Smart Home

40%

21°C
69.8°F

09:37

Security

Lighting

Network

Camera

ON

◀ Internet of Things devices and applications are becoming more popular each day. They allow you to remotely control everything from kitchen appliances to thermostats and security cameras.

INCREASED USE OF FILELESS CYBERATTACKS IN THE U.S.A.

Fileless (macros, script, in-memory)   File-based (exe, doc, bat, dll, hta, pdf, etc.)

20%
80%
2016

29%
71%
2017

35%
65%
2018

The growth of fileless and file-based cyberattacks based on survey of 665 information technology and cybersecurity leaders

Cybercriminals are constantly coming up with new ways to access digital data, so it is important to stay informed and up to date all the time. To keep up with **current affairs**, you must follow daily news, social media, and Internet alerts.

IMPACT OF CYBERCRIME ON INDUSTRY

Damage to business reputation 8%

Lawsuits, fines, regulations 4%

Damage to computer network 10%

Loss of user productivity 30%

Theft of vital information 23%

Computer system unusable 25%

Loss of $300+ per employee
Based on survey of 665 information technology and cybersecurity leaders in the U.S. in 2017

INTERNET SEARCHES

When looking at websites, address extensions can help identify the sources of the information.

.gov (government)—official government organizations or departments. You may not be able to access all areas of these websites.

.org (organization)—usually nonprofit organizations and charities. You may have to register to use these.

.com (commercial)—mostly businesses. It is the most widely used web address extension.

Country extensions:

.ca	Canada
.us	United States
.au	Australia
.uk	United Kingdom
.ru	Russia
.de	Germany

◄ The availability of smartphones has sparked an increase in cyberattacks. These devices are even more vulnerable to attack than laptops or computers, especially since 96 percent of smartphones do not come with pre-installed security software.

YOUR OWN NEWS DIET

The Internet provides a constant flow of information from across the globe, and you can access it whenever it is convenient for you. However, not all online information is created equally. Some information is outdated, false, or contains bias. Social media feeds provide quick and easy access to information, but they offer only a narrow perspective.

It is important to access information from a variety of sources to make sure you understand the big picture. Developing a well-balanced **news diet** is a great way to stay informed. Use these sources to stay informed about digital data security threats and preventive measures:

- Stream fact-based news media on the Internet such as the Cable News Network (CNN) and National Public Radio (NPR).
- Read major newspapers and magazines such as *Time, The New York Times, The Wall Street Journal,* and *USA Today.*
- Talk with friends, family, and teachers about current affairs. Be open to new and different perspectives.
- Watch TV documentaries about the topic.
- Listen to radio interviews, panels, and discussions with workers, employers, business leaders, and politicians about cybersecurity issues.
- Set up a Google alert for news stories about digital data security and cyberattacks.
- Read brochures containing facts and information about cyberthreats.

Many organizations are now using sophisticated security measures to help secure their digital data. Endpoint detection and response (EDR) solutions help companies discover, investigate, and respond to threats across endpoints, or different devices, connected to a system. Deception technologies take the advantage away from the hacker. They are used to create decoy systems within an organization's networks. When a hacker attempts to access a decoy, the organization can observe the attacker's actions and learn from them before shutting down the attack.

WHAT YOU CAN DO

There are many things you can do to protect yourself against cybersecurity threats. Try these techniques:

- Always lock your computer and log out of any programs.
- Create strong passwords and do not share them with anyone.
- Back up your computer systems and devices often.
- Do not click links that look suspicious or end in an unfamiliar extension.
- Do not email credit card numbers or personal information, and ensure online transactions are secure.
- Do not respond to emails asking for money.
- Do not click links or open attachments in unsolicited emails.
- Adjust your privacy settings on social media platforms to ensure strangers cannot access your information.
- Make sure apps are legitimate before downloading or allowing them to access other information on your devices.

ASK YOUR OWN QUESTIONS

Do you think cybercrime can ever be stopped? If so, how? If not, how can we better cope with it?

SEARCH TIPS

In search windows on the Internet:

- Use quotation marks around a phrase to find that exact combination of words (for example, "privacy settings").

- Use the minus sign to eliminate certain words from your search (for example, Digital security -malware).

- Use a colon and an extension to search a specific site (for example, Cybercrime:.gov for all government website mentions of the topic).

- Use the word Define and a colon to search for word definitions (for example, Define: hacker).

STORING PASSWORDS

3%
Use password
management program

2%
Save in
Internet browser

6%
Other methods

6%
Save in note
on computer
or smartphone

18%
Write them on
a piece of paper

65%
Memorize them

Based on survey of 1,040 adult computer users in the United States in 2016

▲ Currently, there are about 25 connected devices per 100 people in the United States. This is likely to increase to 30 devices per 100 people by the year 2020.

43

GLOSSARY

anonymity When a person's name is not known or provided

backups Copies of data that can be used if the originals are damaged

bitcoins A form of electronic cash that is exchanged online without using banks

campaigns Plans with a specific purpose

chief evangelist A person who promotes a specific technology to get people to use it and make it the industry standard

cloud In computing, a shared storage system

complacency Having a sense of security or of being content with a situation because one is not aware of potential dangers

context Circumstances, background, or setting for an event, idea, or activity

credible Able to be trusted or believed

current affairs Events happening now

cybercriminals People who use computers and technology to commit crimes

encryption A method used to convert data into code so that people cannot use or access it without authorization

espionage The act of spying or using spies to learn secrets

evaluating Judging or determining the value of something

evidence Facts or information that prove if something is true or real

firewalls Computer systems designed to block unauthorized users from gaining access

fraud Deceiving or tricking others for personal gain

hardware Physical units of a computer system such as memory chips, storage devices, and scanners

identity theft Gaining access to and using someone's personal information without permission

inhibitions Feelings of embarrassment or fear that keep a person from performing certain actions

Internet of Things Household digital devices that are linked to and can be controlled from the Internet

interpretation Explaining the meaning of something

intrusion Getting into in an underhand way

isolation Being separate from others

machine learning A branch of artificial intelligence (AI) that allows machines to teach themselves and learn from experience

malicious Deliberately harmful or bad

manipulate To handle or control a person or object in order to take advantage of it

mobilize Move into action

myths False beliefs or ideas that people hold true

negligence Failing to take proper care of something

news diet The sources you use to get your news

perspectives Viewpoints

policies Ideas, plans, and procedures used to guide decision making

proactive Taking actions to control a situation and make changes before it happens

protocols Official procedures and rules that explain how something should be done

Republican People who support the Republican Party, which favors the government playing a limited role in economic matters

social engineering Encouraging or persuading people to perform certain actions

social media Websites and computer software that let people communicate and share information

society People living and working together in a country in an organized way

software Computer programs and operating systems

Soviet Union The former Union of Soviet Socialist Republics (U.S.S.R.) that is today the country of Russia

statistics A type of math that deals with the collection, analysis, and presentation of numerical data; also the numerical data itself

summarizing Stating the main points briefly

victim A person who has been harmed, attacked, or injured by someone else

vulnerable Able to be easily controlled or influenced

45

SOURCE NOTES

QUOTATIONS
p. 4: https://www.fbi.gov/news/testimony/homeland-threats-and-the-fbis-response

p. 7: https://www.goodreads.com/quotes/789592-as-the-world-is-increasingly-interconnected-everyone-shares-the-responsibility

p. 11: https://www.cnbc.com/2018/03/21/facebook-ceo-mark-zuckerbergs-statements-on-privacy-2003-2018.html

p. 26: https://www.goodreads.com/author/quotes/17178817.Stephane_Nappo

p. 38: https://www.pbs.org/newshour/show/exit-interview-janet-reno

REFERENCES USED FOR THIS BOOK

Chapter 1: Global Security Risks, pp. 4–7
https://www.cybintsolutions.com/cyber-security-facts-stats/

https://www.websitebuilderexpert.com/us-state-cybercrime-losses/

https://study.com/academy/lesson/what-is-digital-data.html

https://www.cleverism.com/complete-guide-data-security/

https://www.statista.com/topics/2588/us-consumers-and-cyber-crime/

Chapter 2: How to Get Informed, pp. 8–13
https://www.skillsyouneed.com/learn/sources-info.html

http://webapps.national.edu/research_writing/docs/PDFs/Reliability_of_Websites.pdf

http://rasmussen.libanswers.com/faq/32400

https://www.ekransystem.com/en/blog/cyber-security-statistics

https://www.straitstimes.com/opinion/learning-to-see-things-from-anothers-perspective

Chapter 3: The Big Picture, pp. 14–23
https://encyclopedia.kaspersky.com/knowledge/a-brief-history-of-hacking/

https://www.sentinelone.com/blog/history-of-cyber-security/

https://www.infosecurity-magazine.com/opinions/the-history-of-cybersecurity/

https://en.softonic.com/articles/all-about-creeper-the-first-virus-in-history

https://searchnetworking.techtarget.com/definition/ARPANET

https://www.techopedia.com/definition/15450/gray-hat-hacker

Chapter 4: An Informed Decision, pp. 24–35
https://www.tripwire.com/state-of-security/security-awareness/5-social-engineering-attacks-to-watch-out-for/

https://mashable.com/article/facebook-50-million-accounts-hacked/#MyTRtfi4MuqV

https://www.cybintsolutions.com/cyber-security-facts-stats/

https://digitalguardian.com/blog/history-data-breaches

https://www.thesslstore.com/blog/2018-cybercrime-statistics/

https://interwork.com/equifax-cyber-attack-happened-protect/

Chapter 5: Staying Informed, pp. 36–39
https://blog.barkly.com/2018-cybersecurity-statistics

https://www.wired.com/story/2018-worst-hacks-so-far/

https://www.nytimes.com/2018/07/27/us/politics/russian-hackers-electric-grid-elections-.html

https://www.computerweekly.com/news/450432488/Ransomware-to-hit-cloud-computing-in-2018-predicts-MIT

Chapter 6: Plan of Action, pp. 40–43
https://www.forbes.com/sites/danwoods/2018/06/22/how-deception-technology-gives-you-the-upper-hand-in-cybersecurity/#40ee7b79689e

https://www.jisc.ac.uk/blog/how-do-you-keep-students-safe-from-cyber-crime-by-teaching-them-to-behave-like-a-stealth-bomber

FIND OUT MORE

Finding good source material on the Internet can sometimes be a challenge. When analyzing how reliable the information is, consider these points:

- Who is the author of the page? Is it an expert in the field or a person who experienced the event?

- Is the site well known and up to date? A page that has not been updated for several years probably has out-of-date information.

- Can you verify the facts with another site? Always double-check information.

- Have you checked all possible sites? Don't just look on the first page a search engine provides.

- Remember to try government sites and research papers.

- Have you recorded website addresses and names? Keep this data so you can backtrack later and verify the information you want to use.

WEBSITES

Learn how to protect yourself from cyberattacks.
https://www.getcybersafe.gc.ca/index-en.aspx

Get the latest cybersecurity news.
http://www.itsecurityguru.org/

Read the online edition of *Wired*, a monthly magazine about technology and its impact on society.
https://www.wired.com/

Find out how to detect and respond to cyberthreats.
https://www.ready.gov/cybersecurity

BOOKS

Kamar, Haq. *What Is Cybersecurity?* Britannica Educational Publishing, 2018.

Kamberg, Mary-Lane. *Cybersecurity: Protecting Your Identity and Data.* Rosen, 2018.

Lennex, Amy. *Personal Data Management.* Cherry Lake Publishing, 2017.

Loh-Hagan, Virginia. *Ethical Hacker.* 45th Parallel Press, 2015.

ABOUT THE AUTHOR

Heather C. Hudak has written hundreds of books for kids. When she is not writing, she enjoys traveling the world and spending time with her husband and their many rescue cats and dogs.

INDEX